OVERCOMING ADDICTION™

HEROIN, OPIOID, AND PAINKILLER ABUSE

BETHANY BRYAN

Rosen
YA
New York

Published in 2019 by The Rosen Publishing Group, Inc.
29 East 21st Street, New York, NY 10010

First Edition

Library of Congress Cataloging-in-Publication Data

Names: Bryan, Bethany, author.
Title: Heroin, opioid, and painkiller abuse / Bethany Bryan.
Description: New York : Rosen Publishing, 2019. | Series: Overcoming addiction | Audience: Grades 7–12. | Includes bibliographical references and index.
Identifiers: LCCN 2017056405| ISBN 9781508179436 (library bound) | ISBN 9781508179597 (paperback)
Subjects: LCSH: Drug abuse—Juvenile literature. | Heroin abuse—Juvenile literature. | Opioid abuse—Juvenile literature.
Classification: LCC RC564.3 .B79 2019 | DDC 362.29—dc23
LC record available at https://lccn.loc.gov/2017056405

Manufactured in the United States of America

CONTENTS

INTRODUCTION

Those who had worked with him said that Philip Seymour Hoffman could play almost any film role. He'd portrayed an upper crust snob, a tornado-obsessed storm chaser, a nurse witnessing the last hours of a dying patient's life, the charismatic leader of a cult, even author Truman Capote. Outwardly, in early 2014, he was an actor at the height of his career, an Academy Award winner, playing the role of Plutarch Heavensbee in the acclaimed Hunger Games series. But inwardly, Hoffman was battling a demon that he had been fighting for a long time—he had relapsed into a cycle of heroin abuse.

Opioid drugs, including heroin, are among the most addictive drugs, killing an average of ninety Americans per day, according to the Centers for Disease Control (CDC). Additionally, the rates of relapse are extremely high for opioids. A study on DrugAbuse.com shows that 91 percent of participating opioid users reported a relapse after drug treatment—59 percent of these occurred within a week of being discharged from the rehabilitation program. While the illegal use of heroin represents a significant portion of these numbers, some opioid drugs are available by prescription and are often used to treat pain. Many experts have begun referring to the increasing numbers of this type of addiction as the opioid crisis. This crisis has even had a

Actor Philip Seymour Hoffman passed away in 2014 after slipping back into regular opioid abuse. Recovery is a difficult process for many.

significant impact on the economy, driving up health care costs and business expenditures and increasing costs to the criminal justice system by around $5 billion, according to a recent article in the *New Yorker*. And the crisis doesn't appear to be slowing down. According to the CDC, overdose deaths caused by opioids have quadrupled since 1999. Nearly half of these deaths can be attributed to a prescription opioid.

Philip Seymour Hoffman had gotten clean at the age of twenty-two after a long struggle with heroin addiction. He stayed clean for twenty-three years as his career really took off. In May of 2013, however, he checked himself into rehab, struggling with a relapse, even after twenty-three years of sobriety. He left the program after ten days and continued to work, filming a pilot for Showtime. It seemed he had kicked the habit again. But not quite a year later, on February 2, 2014, a worried friend entered Hoffman's apartment to check on him and found the actor dead. Seventy small bags of heroin were found in Hoffman's apartment, but his official cause of death was a dangerous mixture of heroin, cocaine, benzodiazepines (prescription psychoactive drugs), and amphetamine. He was forty-six.

Drug abuse and addiction are sometimes not apparent to outsiders. Opioid addiction is often easy to hide because many people who abuse these types of drugs started off with a legitimate need for pain relief. They might be sick or have an injury that causes chronic pain. Heroin addiction can often be mistaken for fatigue, flu, or even stress to the untrained eye. So how do you recognize the signs of drug abuse in yourself and others? And what can you do in the face of opioid addiction, which claims thousands of lives each year?

In order to answer these questions, it's important to first learn about opioids themselves, the short- and long-term effects of opium-based drugs, how to recognize addiction, and the signs of an overdose. This knowledge will provide you with tools that can help you and those around you navigate the difficult road to recovery.

CHAPTER 1

AN INTRODUCTION TO OPIOIDS

To understand opioids and their impact, one must start first with the history and legacy of opium. Opium is the resin found in a particular species of poppy—the *Papaver somniferum*, often referred to as the opium poppy. This type of poppy was first grown in Mesopotamia around 3400 BCE. The Sumerians called the plant *hul gil,* which translates into "joy plant." It was used for both recreational and medicinal purposes, as opium could be used as a painkiller and sedative and could give users a feeling of euphoria. Over time, the use of opium spread across Asia, eventually finding its way to Europe via the Silk Road, a series of trade routes that allowed for the exchange of goods between Asia and Europe. The opium trade flourished for hundreds of years, becoming a key British import. In 1527, black pills known

There are many, many species of poppy, but the one that opium is made from is the *Papaver somniferum*, often called the opium poppy.

as the "stones of immortality" were introduced and sold as painkillers. They were made up of a combination of opium, citrus juice, and just a hint of gold quintessence. This marked the first introduction of opium sold in the form of laudanum, a small amount of opium mixed with other "medicinal" substances (alcohol, spices, herbs, and chloroform on occasion) and marketed as medicine. But it wasn't until 1803 that a German pharmacist's apprentice by the name of Friedrich Sertuerener neutralized one of the key ingredients of opium. His discovery became known as morphine, named after Morpheus, the Greek god of sleep and dreams.

MORPHINE

Over hundreds of years of study, people have discovered numerous medical uses for opium, but arguably the most important of these discoveries is morphine. Morphine is an analgesic, a pain reliever that does not cause the patient to lose consciousness, ten times more powerful than processed opium itself. During the Civil War, morphine was used to treat pain in soldiers on both sides of the conflict. It remains in use to this day, but only to treat severe pain and under close supervision by a doctor. Morphine is one of the most addictive substances on earth.

CODEINE

In 1832, a French chemist by the name of Jean-Pierre Robiquet isolated another component of opium. Codeine is a pain reliever and often used as a cough suppressant. If you've had a severe cold, you've likely taken Tylenol with codeine, since it's often

Codeine is one component created from opium. It is often used as a pain reliever, sometimes prescribed by doctors in cases of cold and flu.

mixed with acetaminophen. Because it is technically a narcotic, even though it is less powerful than morphine, doctors prescribe codeine very carefully.

PARTIALLY SYNTHETIC OPIOIDS

Drugs—morphine and codeine—that are derived from opium itself are referred to as opiates. But these are collected under the broader term "opioids," which refers to both opiates and synthetic drugs that were created in order to mimic the effects of opiates. Some opioids, however, are both synthetic and opium based. The most widely known of these is heroin.

LAUDANUM AND FAME

During the 1800s, laudanum rose above existing simply as medication and became somewhat fashionable, leading to some very famous cases of addiction.

- Thomas Jefferson used laudanum to cope with some chronic bowel issues and even cultivated a field of poppies for his personal use at Monticello.

- Poet Samuel Taylor Coleridge is said to have composed "Kubla Khan," his most famous work, while under the influence of laudanum.

- Mathematical genius and one of the earliest computer programmers (if not the first) Ada Lovelace was sometimes sick and often ingested laudanum and wine, as prescribed by her doctor.

- First lady Mary Todd Lincoln used laudanum to help her cope with chronic migraines.

- Poet Percy Bysshe Shelley allegedly used laudanum to help him cope with what might have been bipolar disorder. It's unknown, however, whether his wife Mary Shelley, the author of *Frankenstein*, ever used laudanum, but during the early days of writing her most famous work, Mary's stepsister, Fanny Imlay, committed suicide by taking an overdose of laudanum.

HEROIN

Seventy-one years after morphine was first synthesized, British chemist Charles Wright was studying the drug, combining it with a variety of acids, and hoping to find a non-addictive alternative to morphine. The product of his work became known as heroin. Heroin was eight times more powerful than the morphine it was synthesized from. At first, it was hailed as a miracle drug and sold as a cough suppressant. Heroin was given to babies suffering from bronchitis. The name "heroin" was actually a brand name created by the Bayer Company.

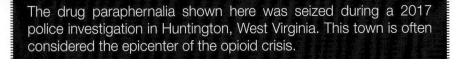

The drug paraphernalia shown here was seized during a 2017 police investigation in Huntington, West Virginia. This town is often considered the epicenter of the opioid crisis.

But in the early 1900s, doctors finally began to acknowledge the signs of heroin addiction in patients. Bellevue, a New York City hospital, admitted its first heroin addict in 1910. Only five years later, 425 heroin-addicted patients were admitted to the hospital. Use of heroin was completely outlawed by 1924 but continues to be made available in the United States through the illegal drug trade.

OXYCODONE

In addition to morphine and codeine, a third substance is synthesized from opium is thebaine. You likely haven't heard of thebaine, but you have heard of oxycodone, which is a drug made from a combination of thebaine and synthetic materials. Oxycodone is a pain medication that is frequently prescribed under the brand name OxyContin. Mixed with acetaminophen, it's commonly prescribed as Percocet.

HYDROCODONE

Hydrocodone, also synthesized from thebaine, is often prescribed for pain falling into the mild or moderate category. You might get a prescription for hydrocodone after a dental surgery under the more familiar brand name Vicodin. Hydrocodone is one of the most widely abused prescription drugs in the United States.

OTHER SEMISYNTHETIC OPIOIDS

Also falling under the category of semisynthetic opioids are hydromorphone, oxymorphone, and buprenorphine.

Hydromorphone and oxymorphone are powerful painkillers, both often available in time-release or instant-release form (making them popular with opioid addicts seeking a quick high) while buprenorphine is often used to help treat opioid addiction.

SYNTHETIC OPIOIDS

The final type of opioids falls under the category of synthetic opioids, containing no actual opium or derivative of opium. These substances are similar in structure to opiates and mimic the effects that opiates have on the body.

MEPERIDINE

Often prescribed under the more familiar name Demerol, meperidine is used to treat severe pain, often before a surgical procedure. But doctors are very careful in how they administer this drug because it can lead to seizures and damage to the central nervous system and tends to not last as long as other pain medications.

FENTANYL

First synthesized in 1960, fentanyl is one hundred times more potent than morphine, so therefore only administered in small doses, and is the most widely prescribed synthetic opioid. Patients are often given fentanyl via a transdermal patch, or a patch that releases small doses over a seventy-two hour period, making it more inconspicuous for abusers. Fentanyl is also often mixed with heroin when sold on the street.

Fentanyl is a synthetic opioid considered more addictive and deadly than heroin. Deaths from fentanyl rose 540 percent in 2016.

METHADONE

The final opioid under the synthetic opioid category is methadone. The most common use for methadone is in the treatment of opioid addiction. When only the prescribed daily dose is ingested, methadone does not allow its user to achieve a high, but blocks the symptoms of opioid withdrawal. Often doctors will adjust dosage many times in order to prevent a patient from developing an addiction to the methadone instead.

CHAPTER 2

OPIOIDS AND THE BODY

Now that we have explored the different types of opioids, let's take a look at what actually happens inside the body when a person takes this type of drug.

OPIOIDS AND THE BRAIN

Everything that happens inside the brain is caused by nerve cells (or neurons) communicating with each other. They communicate through electrical impulses and the release of certain chemicals, called neurotransmitters. On every neuron, you'll find tiny receptors, whose job it is to receive and bond with neurotransmitters. The type of neurotransmitter released helps determine how the brain, and ultimately the body, reacts to a situation. Glutamate is involved in learning, emotion, and thought. Epinephrine helps the body determine how to use glucose during an activity, like exercise. Endorphins give the body the ability to

The neurotransmitter dopamine is the chemical that makes you feel giddy when you have a crush or fall in love. Opioids cause dopamine to be released in the brain at a higher-than-normal rate.

handle pain. But the most important neurotransmitter when it comes to the function of opioids is dopamine.

When dopamine is released and bonds with the appropriate receptor on a neuron, a person will achieve a feeling of pleasure or happiness. Dopamine is the reason you feel giddy when you start to fall in love. Opioids mimic certain neurotransmitters and bond to receptors in the place of the body's natural neurotransmitters, like endorphins. This triggers the body to release dopamine

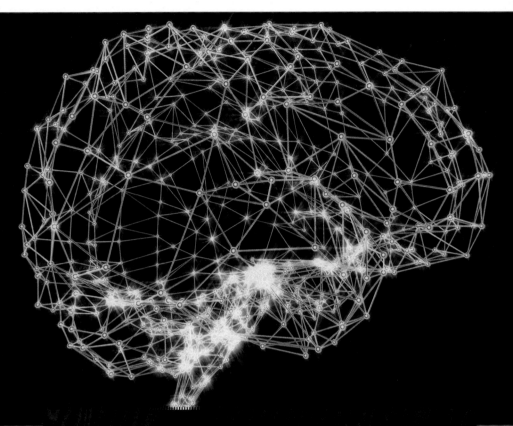

The brain is a network of nerve cells all communicating with one another, often called the neural network. Opioids affect how the cells communicate.

excessively, heightening a person's feeling of pleasure beyond what is normal. People can become addicted to this heightened sense of pleasure and begin to take more and more of the drug in order to achieve the same high. This addiction to pleasure is an addiction to opioids.

THE EFFECTS OF OPIOIDS

One of the most challenging issues in the fight against opioid abuse is that these types of drugs do effectively control pain.

Heroin was brought into the world by a well-meaning chemist who simply wanted to help people before it was discovered that the drug was causing more harm than good. And certain opioids *have* helped people. Morphine has been in use for almost two hundred years, and it has arguably changed how effectively doctors are able to treat pain in patients before, during, and after surgery. Therefore, some of the effects of these types of drugs can be beneficial. Others can be unpleasant side effects, which is why doctors are so careful to monitor patients that are using prescription opioids for pain relief. Let's take a look at some of the effects opioids can have on different parts of the body.

BRAIN AND NERVOUS SYSTEM

When opioids attach themselves to nerve cell receptors, this interrupts the transmission of pain signals and causes the brain to release dopamine. The result is a pleasant, pain-free, euphoric sensation. Under the influence of opioids, one will begin to feel drowsy. If you've ever been to a hospital to visit friends after surgery and they are asleep when you arrive or seem drowsy when they are awake, opioids are likely the reason for this. These short-term effects on the brain are similar for people who abuse prescription painkillers and heroin, but drug abuse exists outside of a controlled environment. No one is there to prevent a user from taking more of the drug, so it's the long-term effects on the brain that become more of an issue over time. In the long term, chronic pain that has been overtreated with opioids can actually intensify, which can result in increased substance abuse. Opioids can also lead to psychomotor impairment, which means that the body physically slows down over time and loses coordination. Overuse and abuse of opioids in the long term can also lead to lethargy (chronic tiredness) or heightened bouts of depression.

RESPIRATORY AND CIRCULATORY SYSTEM

As opioids begin to take effect in the body, they actually slow down the respiratory system. The brain handles all passive functions in the body. You don't have to actively tell yourself to breathe every few seconds because the brain does that for you. But under the influence of opioids, the brain "forgets." If you're sleep deprived when you're trying to take a test, you won't do as well as if you got eight hours of sleep the night before. The brain reacts similarly while under the influence of opioids. This means that the body breathes more slowly, taking in less oxygen. If less oxygen than normal is reaching the brain and other vital organs, this can result in permanent damage. Under the right circumstances, whether someone is using opioids in the short or long term, this can result in unconsciousness, coma, or even death.

Long-term effects on the respiratory and circulatory systems can also be determined by the method by which someone takes the drug. Many drug users choose to dissolve opioids and inject them because the drugs take effect more quickly than swallowing a pill, resulting in a more intense high. But small particles are not as small as red blood cells and have trouble passing through vein walls. This can lead to infection in the areas around the heart, damage to the veins, and pulmonary embolism—a blockage of a blood vessel in the lung. Drug users who smoke opioids achieve a similar fast-acting effect to injecting the drugs. Smoking can also make drug use more inconspicuous since long-term injections can leave marks on the body. But smoking can cause damage to the lungs, in addition to slowing respiration.

HOW MUCH MORPHINE IN A MUFFIN?

If morphine is derived from poppy seeds and we eat poppy seeds in bagels, cakes, muffins, and other baked goods, are we actually ingesting morphine? The answer is yes, but it's not enough to really affect you ... unless you seriously overeat. There are a wide variety of poppies, and the seeds contain different amounts of morphine. The Spanish poppy actually contains the most morphine at around 251 micrograms per gram of poppy seeds. The average dose of morphine given during or after a medical procedure is between 10 and 30 milligrams. An average recipe for poppy seed muffins calls for only about 2 tablespoons (28.3 grams) of poppy seeds in order to yield twenty-four muffins of average

(continued on the next page)

Poppy seeds contain trace amounts of opium, but not enough to cause any significant effect—unless you eat way too many of them!

(continued from the previous page)

size, meaning that there are only about 7.1 milligrams of morphine in the entire batch. In order to get a minimum dose (10 milligrams), you would have to eat around thirty-three whole average-sized poppy seed muffins and a little bit of a thirty-fourth. And that's only if you're using the most potent poppy seeds available!

DIGESTIVE SYSTEM

In the same way that lung function slows down when a person is under the influence of an opioid, passive digestive function can slow down as well, resulting in severe constipation and bloating. Opioids can also cause nausea and vomiting by irritating the stomach or affecting the inner ear, which can make you dizzy.

Over time, someone who abuses opioids might develop a small bowel obstruction, tears in the intestine walls, inflammation, and even sepsis, which ties in to immune system response.

IMMUNE SYSTEM

When infection-causing agents—bacteria, fungi, viruses, or parasites—enter the body, the immune system responds by releasing leukocytes (or white blood cells) whose job it is to destroy them. They also work to create antibodies, which help prevent similar infection in the future. At least that's how it's supposed to work. But when someone is under the influence of opioids, the immune system doesn't react the way it's supposed to because it's not receiving the important information from the brain that the body is under attack. It can even begin attacking parts of the body itself, rather than the invading pathogens, a

When you're sick, your immune system goes to work eradicating the invading virus or bacteria. But under the influence of opioids, your body struggles to react the way it should.

condition known as sepsis. Sometimes called "blood poisoning," sepsis can lead to the body's natural defenses causing damage and shutting down organs.

LIVER FUNCTION

Many opioids, hydrocodone (Vicodin) for instance, are combined with acetaminophen, the pain reliever found in Tylenol. Overuse of acetaminophen can actually result in liver damage over a long period of time.

THE RISK OF OVERDOSE

An overdose can happen to anyone—both experienced drug users and first-time users. Overdose occurs when an individual consumes more of a substance than his or her body has the ability to manage. In order to save a life, it's important to understand the risk factors for overdose, how to recognize one, and what to do in case of an overdose.

OVERDOSE RISK FACTORS

There are four heightened risk factors that can potentially lead to an overdose. If you or someone you know is at increased risk for overdose, don't wait to seek help.

- Tolerance. As the body adapts to a drug and eventually comes to require it in order to function, a drug user will start to use more and more in order to achieve the same effects. Not having a set limit on what the body can tolerate means that it's easier to go past that limit.
- Mixing. Drugs like heroin already slow response time and function of the body. Adding another depressant, like alcohol, increases the danger of overdose and unconsciousness. Mixing heroin with a stimulant, like cocaine (often called speedballing), decreases the sedative effects of heroin, often making the user feel less affected, causing him or her to take more.
- Method. Injecting, smoking, or snorting an opioid can lead to a faster high than ingesting a pill and allowing the body to metabolize it. This heightens the risk of overdose.

- Relapse. Once you've kicked the habit, your body is no longer used to a dosage that it once found normal. This increases the chance of overdose if you pick up your old habit.

RECOGNIZING AN OVERDOSE AND GETTING HELP

On overdose can be recognized by a number of factors, including unconsciousness that the person cannot be roused

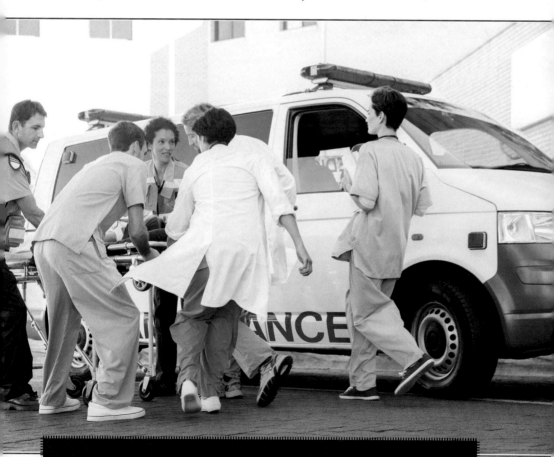

Ambulances often carry doses of naloxone, a drug that can rapidly reverse the effects of an opioid overdose if delivered in time.

from; decreased breathing, often represented by bluish lips or fingernails; pinpoint pupils; pale, clammy skin; and vomiting.

If you fear that you're experiencing an overdose, find a place to sit down, keep yourself propped upright (or lie down on your side), and call 911 right away. Unfortunately, opioids often work too quickly for you to personally understand that you're in danger and reach out for help.

If you suspect that someone you know is overdosing, it's important to act quickly. Call 911 immediately. As you're waiting for help to arrive, help the person to sit upright and monitor their breathing. If they stop breathing, administer CPR. If they vomit, roll them onto their side so that they don't choke. Although you might be afraid of getting into trouble yourself, if your friend's life is in danger, you'll need to be as honest as possible with 911 dispatch and the EMTs. They need to know how to deliver help.

MYTHS AND FACTS

MYTH: Opioid addicts are bad, selfish people.

FACT: We often see drug addicts portrayed negatively in the media, but many people who suffer from opioid addiction were simply seeking relief from pain and discovered that they couldn't stop taking the drug. Others use drugs to avoid mental anguish or to simply have a new experience. Addiction can lead to selfish, dangerous behavior, but that does not make the addict a bad person.

MYTH: Only people who exhibit an "addictive personality" have to worry about addiction.

FACT: While certain genetic and social factors make some individuals more likely to abuse drugs, anyone can develop an addiction under the right circumstances.

MYTH: It is impossible to recover from heroin addiction.

FACT: While heroin and other opioids have a high percentage of relapse cases, with the right support and a good treatment program, complete recovery is possible with time, support, and a lot of hard work.

CHAPTER 3

RECOGNIZING ADDICTION

One of the biggest misconceptions about drug addiction is that it is caused by weakness, or a character flaw in the drug user. Many believe that if the person can just employ some willpower and stop using, everything will be fine. But this belief does not speak to the underlying reasons for drug addiction and abuse, which are often ignored. Many doctors and mental health professionals are trying to change this stigma of drug abuse as weakness and recognize it instead as a disease. This would allow addicts to receive care and support for addiction in the same way they might for any physical ailment that requires medical attention. To fully understand addiction, however, it's important to start with *why* addiction occurs.

WHY PEOPLE ABUSE OPIOIDS

People may begin to use opioids for a variety of reasons. Some enjoy the thrill of trying a new experience. Others find that drugs

People abuse drugs for a lot of reasons, and one of the keys to recovery is discovering your own reasons. Group therapy helps a lot of addicts every year.

provide relief from some of the stress in their lives. One of the keys to battling addiction is understanding how it began. Let's look at some more reasons why people may be struggling with addiction.

PAIN RELIEF

Opioid addicts may have started with a legitimate need for pain relief and then couldn't quite kick the habit when the prescription

Former Packers quarterback Brett Favre struggled with an addiction to Vicodin after a series of surgeries. Luckily, with lots of support, he was able to recover.

ran out. During his time as a National Football League (NFL) quarterback, Brett Favre struggled with addiction to Vicodin. He had been suffering for years with pain caused by past injuries and surgeries. At one point he was taking fifteen of the pills at a time. In 1996, at the height of his addiction, Favre suffered a seizure after a routine ankle surgery because of his abuse of the narcotic. At that point, he knew he needed help and entered a rehabilitation program with the help and support of the NFL.

Eighties heartthrobs Corey Haim (*right*) and Corey Feldman *(left)* both struggled with addiction after suffering childhood trauma. Feldman recovered, but Haim passed away in 2010.

SELF-MEDICATION

Others who abuse opioids might try them as a means to self-medicate following mental or physical trauma, or social issues like anxiety, depression, and stress. Actor Corey Feldman, who rose to fame in the 1980s as a child actor, starring in films like *Stand By Me* and *The Goonies,* struggled with heroin addiction for years after he was sexually abused by a family friend. He entered into rehab in 1990 and has remained clean since. However, fellow child actor and close friend Corey Haim died in 2010 of pneumonia caused by prescription pill addiction, which included OxyContin. Haim had also been the victim of sexual abuse as a child.

GENETICS

There are also genetic factors that can lead specific people down the path to addiction. Some addicts are simply more prone to addiction because of "addiction genes" that scientists are still trying to understand. Actor Martin Sheen, famous for roles in *Apocalypse Now* and *The West Wing*, is an alcoholic who has been in recovery for over twenty years. The actor's son, Charlie Sheen, also struggled with alcohol addiction, in addition to issues with cocaine and other drugs.

EARLY EXPOSURE TO DRUGS

Often closely linked to genetic factors, many drug users pick up drug use after exposure to drugs as children or teens, sometimes

Former child star and current actress and producer Drew Barrymore grew up around drug use and fell into the cycle of addiction as a young teen.

by parents or other family members. When actress Drew Barrymore (*E.T., Never Been Kissed, The Wedding Singer*) was nine years old, her mother started taking her to nightclubs, including Studio 54, several nights a week. By thirteen, Barrymore was struggling with addiction to drugs and alcohol, entering a rehab program before she was a year into her teens. Children are often very susceptible to drug abuse because the adults around them normalize the behavior.

RECOGNIZING ADDICTION

Chances are, if you're reading the accompanying sections, you are beginning to recognize that someone you know might be struggling with addiction. The most important thing to understand is that it isn't your fault. People don't become addicted to opioids because you let them down in some way. If you're concerned about a friend or family member's well-being and you're concerned that they might be struggling with opioid addiction, take a look at some of the signs.

Physically, your loved one might be acting strange, drowsy, or happy at odd moments. They might be struggling to stay awake at times or sleeping more often than usual. Some nonphysical signs include going to the doctor more frequently and bringing home prescription meds more often. They might suffer from mood swings. Your loved one might pull away emotionally and seem to want to be left alone. They might bring up sudden financial issues that weren't a problem in the past.

If you notice a number of these factors, you have every right to feel concerned. If the loved one is a parent and you feel anxious about speaking to them personally, try to find another family member or other trusted adult who may be able to listen, understand, and potentially intervene on your behalf. It's OK to ask for help. If you're worried that your friend or loved one might get in trouble and are afraid to reach out to others, you might try getting in contact with a drug abuse hotline in your area. There are also groups like Al-Anon, where family members of addicts can come together in a group setting for support. Look online for similar groups in your area. If you're afraid to go alone, ask someone to go with you.

YOUR OWN ADDICTION

If the substance abuse issues you're worried about are your own, one of the first steps is to recognize that you might have a problem. And if you're reading this, you've done that. Next, ask yourself some important questions and be honest about the answers.

1. In the past month, have you been to the doctor's office or emergency room more than once?
2. In the past thirty days, have you taken more than your prescribed dosage of medication or used it for any reason that is unrelated to your physical well-being, like falling asleep at night or getting you through a challenging day?
3. Have you taken anyone else's prescribed pain medication?
4. In the past month, has anyone expressed concern over your use of drugs, either prescription or nonprescription?
5. Have you recently started avoiding social activities or interactions with loved ones?
6. Do you experience cravings for the drug or spend time trying to figure out how to acquire more?

7. If you stop taking the drug, do you experience symptoms of withdrawal, like anxiety, restlessness, runny eyes or nose, sweating excessively, or insomnia? (After a few days, these symptoms might turn into abdominal cramping, diarrhea, nausea, blurry vision, or rapid heartbeat.)

If you were able to answer yes to more than one of these questions, opioid addiction might be a concern for you. The good news is that there are ways to get help. We'll discuss recovery options in more detail in a later section, but before planning out your path to recovery, there are a few important things you should do.

First, tell someone. A strong support base is important to recovery, and chances are you've been struggling to find the words to express to someone that you might be in trouble. You might be embarrassed or don't want to be an inconvenience. But now is the time to set that aside and reach out to someone else for help. If your chosen confidante cares about you, they will want to help. You might feel, at first, that they are upset with you. People face a myriad of emotions when it comes to an admission of drug use, and some of these emotions include anger, sadness, or disappointment. But you'll realize that it is better to have someone—even if that someone is momentarily disappointed in you—in your corner rather than face your issues alone. If you don't feel that you have a parent, friend, or other trusted individual with which to share, you still don't have to face your issues alone. Check online for drug addiction support groups in your area or call a drug abuse hotline. You can often remain anonymous for as long as it takes for you to feel comfortable. Often you can find support from someone who has dealt with similar issues.

Once you've spoken to a trusted individual and have started to build a support base, you should next make an appointment with a doctor. Drugs can cause a lot of damage to the body, and some of it might not be immediately apparent. That's why it's important to get checked out. Plus, a doctor can help you start planning your recovery.

If you feel comfortable making an appointment with your family or regular doctor, start there. There is a stigma surrounding drug abuse, and some physicians will not feel comfortable speaking to you about addiction, but don't let that dishearten you. Ask for a referral to a different doctor or a therapist who specializes in addiction and make an appointment.

If you don't have health insurance, there are often clinics that provide care to people on a sliding scale or free of charge. Check online for clinics in your area. You might experience a bit of a wait at free clinics, so bring a supportive friend or something to help occupy your mind, like a notebook for jotting down your feelings, some music, or a book.

During this visit, it's important to be completely honest with the doctor about what you're experiencing. Be prepared to list any and all substances you've been abusing and for how long. Doctors are bound by doctor/patient confidentiality, so, by law, they can't report you to the police for drug abuse. The only exception to this is if they are afraid you might cause harm to yourself or someone else.

CHAPTER 4

THE OPIOID CRISIS AND THE WAR ON DRUGS

After the Civil War, which killed around 620,000 soldiers, an estimated 400,000 soldiers went home, carrying with them a then misunderstood "soldier's disease." Pain management was still a new concept in the 1860s, and amputations and other types of injuries ran rampant during the violent conflict. Morphine was still a pretty new medication, a "miracle drug" that relieved pain and allowed the afflicted to sleep. So doctors treated many of these soldiers both on the battlefield and in hospitals for their pain without too much concern for the long-term effects. The "soldier's disease" was morphine addiction.

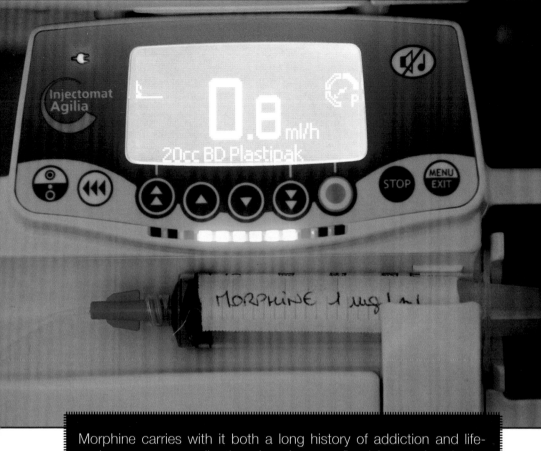

Morphine carries with it both a long history of addiction and life-saving use as a medication since it was refined from opium in the nineteenth century.

Today, morphine is a carefully prescribed medication, only available by prescription in cases of extreme pain, and even then doctors closely monitor its use. But after the Civil War, one could simply order a dose from the Sears and Roebuck catalog. It even came with a syringe!

The ease of availability of drugs in the late 1800s and early 1900s took casual drug use to crisis levels. And the reaction to this crisis would go on to set the course for all drug legislation over the next century and beyond.

EARLY LEGISLATION

By 1908, President Theodore Roosevelt knew that something needed to be done about the drug crisis, particularly the issue with opium. In response, he appointed a doctor named Hamilton Wright to the position of Opium Commissioner. Opium consumption and trade was not exclusively an American issue. Countries across the globe were starting to feel the strain of rampant addiction. In 1909, the Shanghai Opium Commission took place in China, allowing representatives from countries around the world to meet and try to find a solution. Hamilton Wright represented the United States, with the hopes of cutting off the opium trade. But not all countries were on board with that idea. Great Britain had been enjoying a very profitable opium trade with India for hundreds of years. It was beginning to look like there wouldn't be an easy solution to the crisis. But in 1912, representatives met again at The Hague and created the first international opium agreement, which sought to cut off unregulated opium supplies globally. Of course, this didn't stop the illegal opium trade.

Back in the United States in 1913, the government enacted one of the first pieces of legislation in what would become America's war on drugs. The Harrison Act put a tax on the import, manufacture, and sale of drugs, particularly opioids and cocaine. This led to crackdowns on doctors who were previously able to prescribe opiates to patients. Many were imprisoned. Patients who had formerly had access to maintenance doses of the drugs were suddenly cut off and faced dangerous withdrawal symptoms. They were no longer patients. They were criminals. These addicts were forced to seek drugs through illegal means.

In addition to the danger of addiction, now addicts were facing legal consequences *and* the dangers of acquiring unregulated and unlimited doses of drugs from dealers on the street. Suffering only increased during this time.

ANSLINGER AND THE FBN

The Federal Bureau of Narcotics (FBN) was formed in 1930, and a man named Harry Anslinger was named the commissioner

Harry Anslinger, former head of the Federal Bureau of Narcotics, is considered the father of the modern drug war. In particular, he focused his efforts on the criminalization of marijuana.

of the organization. The FBN determined that simply cracking down on drugs like opiates and cocaine wasn't enough. Laws needed to be tightened around all drug use, including marijuana. Sentences for drug offenders needed to be stiffened. Selling heroin to a minor could result in the death penalty under the FBN's new rules.

The FBN also sought to defame certain types of drugs to the public in order to decrease their popularity. To do this, they created propaganda that blamed drugs for sex crimes, murder, and mental illness.

Race was also a big factor in the FBN's new drug policies. Anslinger believed that drug use among the black and Latino communities was dangerous to the rest of American society. He even began a crusade against African-American jazz singer Billie Holiday, who struggled with heroin addiction, taking away her license to perform in clubs in New York. Holiday would later succumb to the long-term effects of drug and alcohol addiction.

NIXON'S WAR ON DRUGS

By the 1960s—despite the efforts of the Federal Bureau of Narcotics—drugs were more popular than ever. Drug references popped up in songs and in popular culture. Marijuana came into fashion on college campuses. Hallucinogens were all the rage as young people sought to "expand their minds." And none of this was going unnoticed by the US government.

By 1971, President Richard Nixon declared a war on drugs, calling drugs public enemy number one. In 1973, he created the Drug Enforcement Agency (DEA). The first mission of the DEA was to tighten the southern border of the United States to prevent

President Ronald Reagan and First Lady Nancy Reagan worked hard to reinforce American antidrug policies during the 1980s. Young people were told to "Just say no!"

drugs from flowing in from Mexico. But as drugs were cut off from Mexico, more began to arrive from Colombia. Under new policies, drug offenders received mandatory prison sentences, which did little to treat the addiction.

Racism was also a component of Nixon's drug policies. According to Nixon adviser John Ehrlichman, the war on drugs was about cracking down on the black community and those who were against the war in Vietnam. He said, in an interview with *Harper's* magazine that was conducted twenty-two years before it was published, "We could arrest their leaders, raid their homes, break up their meetings, and vilify them night after night on the evening news. Did we know we were lying about the drugs? Of course we did."

Ronald Reagan was elected president in 1980 and immediately began to reinforce many of Nixon's antidrug policies. Antidrug messages even entered pop culture as first lady Nancy Reagan spearheaded the "Just Say No" campaign, which gave a popular slogan to the message. Those on the side of the drug war were convinced that stricter policies that cut off drug availability and imposed punishment for drug use and possession were key to curbing drug abuse. Those who spoke out against the drug war argued that this only helped the illegal drug trade since people would do what they needed to do to keep using. Treating addiction as an ailment was far more effective than prosecution, which often leads many people to use drugs again. Both sides of this argument continue today.

DRUG SCHEDULING

Drugs are categorized according to five different schedules. These categories determine how dangerous and addictive the drug might be and also help prosecute drug-related crimes, based on where the drug in question falls within the schedules.

Schedule I: These types of drugs have absolutely no medical use and carry a potential for abuse. The only opioid that falls into this category

(continued on the next page)

(continued from the previous page)

is heroin. Schedule I drugs also include LSD, marijuana, ecstasy, methaqualone (Quaaludes), and peyote. Possession of these types of drugs is a felony.

Schedule II: These types of drugs carry a high potential for abuse and addiction and are considered dangerous. However, they can be prescribed under a doctor's careful supervision. Schedule II opioids include hydrocodone, methadone, hydromorphone, fentanyl, oxycodone, codeine, and meperidine. Other drugs in this category include cocaine, methamphetamine, and certain types of amphetamine frequently used to treat attention deficit hyperactivity disorder (ADHD). Possessing drugs in the Schedule II to Schedule IV categories without a valid prescription is a felony.

Schedule III: These types of drugs tend to not be as addictive as Schedule I or II drugs and are more frequently prescribed by doctors. The only opioid in this category is codeine, which you may remember is also listed as a Schedule II drug. This isn't a mistake! When mixed with acetaminophen, codeine is categorized as a Schedule III drug. Other Schedule III drugs include ketamine, anabolic steroids, and testosterone.

Schedule IV: These types of drugs carry only a low potential for addiction and abuse. Many drugs fall under this category, but some of them include Xanax, Darvocet, Valium, and Ambien. A prescription is required for these drugs.

Schedule V: These types of drugs carry almost no potential for abuse and can be bought over the counter. When mixed with certain medications like guaifenesin and in very small amounts, as in the cough medicine Robitussin, codeine falls under this category.

THE MODERN WAR ON DRUGS

In 1980, around 41,000 individuals were jailed for drug-related crimes. That number increased to 488,400 by 2014, according to Politifact. Currently, about half of US prisoners were incarcerated on drug crimes. Racial disparity continues to be apparent in current rates of incarceration. African Americans represent, according to the National Association for the Advancement of Colored People (NAACP), only 12.5 percent of illicit drug users but are arrested and incarcerated at a higher rate for drug offenses. Twenty-nine percent of people arrested for drug offenses are African American, while 33 percent of those in prison for drug offenses are African American.

SAFEGUARDING YOURSELF

The bottom line is that no matter your feelings toward current US drug policies, to use, be in possession of drugs or drug paraphernalia, sell, or manufacture drugs is illegal. You could spend time in prison and, once released, face the long-term repercussions of a felony conviction, which can make it harder to find a job and limit your personal freedoms. If you are concerned that someone you know might be breaking the law, and you feel comfortable speaking honestly with this individual, share your concerns with him or her. If you aren't comfortable or fear for your safety, go to a trusted adult and do what you can to keep yourself away from the situation. Your safety and well-being should be your top concern.

CHAPTER 5

RECOVERY FROM OPIOID ADDICTION

Whether you've come to terms with your own issues with opioid addiction or are concerned about someone you love, you've probably come to understand that the next step is recovery. Breaking an addiction, however, is not as simple as just quitting. There are physical symptoms of withdrawal that require care from a doctor. The brain is hardwired to addiction as well, so long-term therapy and sometimes medication are also important. Recovery is different for everyone, and there are a lot of different types of drug treatment programs. The first step is finding the right program.

TYPES OF RECOVERY PROGRAMS

When the subject of drug addiction pops up on a TV show or movie, the type of drug treatment program portrayed is often a

In August 2017, protestors gathered outside police headquarters in New York City to protest drug arrests. Many believe that a better approach to addiction is treatment, not punishment.

luxury long-term residential program. You'll often see residents talking in group therapy or attending a yoga session at what looks like a resort. The other characters go on with their lives. And then a title card flashes "A few months later..." and the character, now fully recovered from drug addiction, returns looking happier, healthier, and talking about self-actualization. But this type of program can be very expensive, sometimes running into the hundreds of thousands of dollars. Long-term residential programs are very rarely luxurious, but they can be effective if this is the right type of program for you. The length of a stay in a long-term residential program ranges from between a month and a year. And during that time, addicts focus 100 percent of their energy on recovery, attending therapy and focusing on wellness while spending time away from drugs and drug triggers. The downside of this type of program is that it can be expensive, and you must spend a significant period of time away from family and friends.

There are also short-term residential treatment programs, usually running only twenty-eight to thirty days. These programs can help you through the difficult, dangerous withdrawal period and put you on a path toward making better choices through therapy sessions. The downside of this type of program is that it can still be pretty expensive, despite the shorter stay, but also the direct support period is shortened. If you choose a short-term program, be sure to follow it up with therapy sessions with a counselor trained in addiction treatment.

Outpatient care might be a good option for those who can't or prefer not to spend time away from family or a job. In these types of programs, those in recovery live at home, but must check in to a treatment center several times a week to receive intensive counseling and medication, such as methadone. (During the withdrawal period, opioid addicts are often given methadone to help them cope with symptoms.) Outpatient programs tend to be less expensive than residential programs. The downsides of this type of program are that they require a huge amount of support from family and friends and a large amount of dedication on the part of the addict.

Finally, there is group or individual counseling. If you choose to take this option, you must first find a detox program to help you through withdrawal. Do not try to simply stop using an opioid. The symptoms of withdrawal can be unbearable and even lead to using again. Medical detox programs help patients through the process with medication or slowly stepping down maintenance doses of the drug. Talk to a doctor or therapist about available detox programs near you before trying to kick the habit yourself. Post-detox, you'll want to focus on long-term care through therapy. Group sessions are often free and available through local programs so check online for sessions taking place in your area. If you feel more comfortable speaking to a private counselor, look for therapists trained in this type of care through your insurance program or check online for free or low-cost counseling programs. Twelve-step programs like Narcotics Anonymous or Heroin Anonymous also exist to provide support to recovering addicts, as well as Alcoholics Anonymous. Many AA meetings are drug focused and can provide a great deal of support, even if your addiction isn't to alcohol.

Loved ones of addicts might also benefit from group or individual counseling. There are also programs like Al-Anon and Alateen, which are twelve-step programs geared toward helping family members and loved ones recover from the pain and codependency that often surround addiction.

SELF-CARE AND RECOVERY

As you or your loved one begin the process of recovering from addiction, it's important to remember to be kind to yourself. It can be very easy to turn anger, fear, and frustration inward or even punish yourself for your own addiction or for not acting sooner to help a loved one. These are all totally normal feelings, and therapy,

Many people use journaling or writing to help aid in their recovery from drug addiction. Everyone approaches recovery differently!

or even just talking to a trusted friend, can often help you to examine them more closely. Grab a notebook and write down some things that you would like to focus on to help you cope. Some people like to revisit an old childhood hobby that once brought them joy or seek out a new hobby. Others take up journaling or writing about their experiences. Even just taking a nap can help at times. Recovery isn't an easy process, but with the right tools, it can be an effective one.

TEN GREAT QUESTIONS
TO ASK A DRUG COUNSELOR

1. What is the best type of treatment for my type of opioid addiction?

2. Does this treatment include care during detoxification?

3. Will I be able to see and communicate with family and friends during treatment?

4. Is this treatment program covered by my insurance and/or is there a payment plan available?

5. What kind of support can I expect from this program once I've completed treatment?

6. What happens if I relapse?

7. Is individual or group counseling available?

8. Will I have to take medications to help with my recovery?

9. Are the medications safe?

10. When will I know I've recovered from drug abuse?

GLOSSARY

ADDICTION A condition that is the result of substance abuse or an activity that leaves an individual unable to quit.

CODEINE One of the drugs refined from opium, often used to treat minor pain when paired with Tylenol.

DOPAMINE A neurotransmitter responsible for good feelings in the body.

FELONY The most serious type of crime, often resulting in prison time.

FENTANYL A synthetic opioid painkiller, often ingested via a transdermal patch.

HEROIN A semisynthetic opioid made from morphine that is highly addictive and illegal in the United States.

HYDROCODONE A semisynthetic opioid often prescribed under the names Vicodin or Percocet.

LAUDANUM A mixture of opium, alcohol, and other substances that was fashionable to ingest as medicine during the Victorian era.

LETHARGY A chronic lack of energy or sleepiness.

MORPHINE Refined from opium, this painkiller has been used by doctors for over two hundred years.

NEUROTRANSMITTER Chemicals released in the brain that help the different parts of the body communicate with each other.

OPIATES Opium-based drugs, containing no synthetic materials.

OPIOIDS The collective term for all opiates and any synthetic or partially synthetic drugs used in the place of opiates.

OPIUM   Resin taken from the *Lachryma papaveris* poppy, often used in the production of painkillers.

OVERDOSE   Ingestion of a drug to levels beyond what the body can process.

PAINKILLER   Medications that help alleviate pain.

REHABILITATION   The process of reducing dependency on drug substances through medical treatment or therapy.

SCHEDULE   A government list that separates drugs by the seriousness of their effects and addictive nature.

SPEEDBALLING   The abuse of heroin and cocaine together.

SYNTHETIC   Drugs refined from chemicals, as opposed to natural ingredients.

TOLERANCE   The ability of the body to handle more and more drug substances over time, leading to increased use.

TRANSDERMAL   The application of a drug so that it absorbs through the skin, as in a patch that releases the drug gradually.

FOR MORE INFORMATION

Addiction Center
Recovery Worldwide LLC
121 South Orange Avenue, Suite 1450
Orlando, FL 32801
(877) 416-1550
Website: https://www.addictioncenter.com
Facebook: @TheAddictionCenter
Twitter: @AddictionCentr
Addiction Center is an online guide to help those struggling with
    addiction find help.

Canadian Centre on Substance Use and Addiction (CCSA)
500-75 Albert Street
Ottawa, ON K1P 5E7
Canada
(613) 235-4048
Website: http://www.ccsa.ca
Twitter: @CCSACanada
CCSA works to address issues related to substance abuse and

D. A. R. E. is an in-school education program to help students avoid drugs and other risky circumstances in their lives.

Drug Free America Foundation (DFAF)
5999 Central Avenue, Suite 301
Saint Petersburg, FL 33710
(727) 828-0211
Website: https://dfaf.org
Facebook: @DrugFreeAmericaFndn
Twitter: @DrugFreeAmerica
Drug Free America Foundation is a drug prevention program that helps to develop policies that block illegal drug use and addiction.

Drug Free Kids Canada (DFK Canada)
PO Box 23103
Toronto, ON M5N 3A8
Canada
(416) 479-6972
Website: https://www.drugfreekidscanada.org
Facebook: @DrugFreeKidsCanada
Twitter: @DrugFreeKidsCda
Drug Free Kids Canada offers guidance to parents of teens dealing with drug abuse issues and works with agencies to produce antidrug content.

Hazelden Betty Ford Foundation
PO Box 11
Center City, MN 55012-0011
(866) 296-7404
Website: http://www.hazeldenbettyford.org

Facebook: @hazeldenbettyfordfoundation

Twitter: @hazldnbettyford

The Hazelden Betty Ford Foundation is the largest nonprofit drug and alcohol addiction treatment center in the United States.

National Institute on Drug Abuse (NIDA)

Office of Science Policy and Communications

Public Information and Liaison Branch

6001 Executive Boulevard

Room 5213, MSC 9561

Bethesda, MD 20892

(301) 443-1124

Website: https://www.drugabuse.gov

Facebook: @NIDANIH

Twitter: @NIDAnews

NIDA is a scientific research institute operating under the US Department of Health and Human Services that works to research drug abuse and addiction, prevention, and drug treatment.

FOR FURTHER READING

Barnes, Henrietta Robin, MD. *Hijacked Brains: The Experience and Science of Chronic Addiction*. Hanover, NH: Dartmouth, 2015.

Barnett, Robin. *Addict in the House: A No-Nonsense Family Guide Through Addiction and Recovery*. Oakland, CA: New Harbinger, 2016.

Block, Stanley H., Carolyn Bryant Block, and Guy du Plessis. *Mind-Body Workbook for Addiction: Effective Tools for Substance-Abuse Recovery and Relapse Prevention*. Oakland, CA: New Harbinger, 2016.

Gammill, Joani. *Painkillers, Heroin, and the Road to Sanity: Real Solutions for Long-Term Recovery from Opiate Addiction*. Center City, MN: Hazelden Publishing, 2014.

Greek, Joe. *Coping With Opioid Abuse* (Coping). New York, NY: Rosen Publishing, 2018.

Kerrigan, Michael. *The War on Drugs*. Broomall, PA: Mason Crest, 2017.

Mitchell, Tracey Helton. *The Big Fix: Hope After Heroin*. Berkeley, CA: Seal Press, 2017.

Quinones, Sam. *Dreamland: The True Tale of America's Opiate Epidemic*. New York, NY: Bloomsbury Press, 2015.

Scott, Celicia. *Hard Drugs: Cocaine, LSD, PCP, & Heroin* (Downside of Drugs). Broomall, PA: Mason Crest, 2014.

Szalavitz, Maia. *Unbroken Brain: A Revolutionary New Way of Understanding Addiction*. New York, NY: St. Martin's Press, 2016.

BIBLIOGRAPHY

Adams, Cydney. "The Man Behind the Marijuana Band for All the Wrong Reasons." CBS News, November 17, 2016. https://www.cbsnews.com/news/harry-anslinger-the-man-behind-the-marijuana-ban.

Bellum, Sara. "Real Teens Ask: What Are the Different Types of Opioids?" NIDA for Teens, July 16, 2014. https://teens.drugabuse.gov/blog/post/real-teens-ask-what-are-different-types-opioids-0.

Benson, Thor. "The History of Opium in the United States." attn:, June 14, 2015. https://www.attn.com/stories/1934/why-is-opium-illegal.

Brande, Lauren. "Opioid Overdose." DrugAbuse.com. Retrieved September 20, 2017. https://drugabuse.com/library/opioid-overdose.

Brinson, Will. "Brett Favre Says He Used to Take a Month's Worth of Painkillers in Two Days." CBS Sports, July 30, 2016. https://www.cbssports.com/nfl/news/brett-favre-says-he-used-to-take-a-months-worth-of-painkillers-in-two-days.

Carroll, Lauren. "How the War on Drugs Affected Incarceration Rates." Politifact, July 10, 2016. http://www.politifact.com/truth-o-meter/statements/2016/jul/10/cory-booker/how-war-drugs-affected-incarceration-rates.

Centers for Disease Control and Prevention. "Prescription Opioid Overdose Data." Retrieved September 20, 2017. https://www.cdc.gov/drugoverdose/data/overdose.html.

DEA Museum. "Cannabis, Coca, & Poppy: Nature's Addictive Plants." Retrieved September 21, 2017. https://www.deamuseum.org/ccp/opium/history.html.

Diniejko, Andrzej. "Victorian Drug Use." Victorian Web. Retrieved September 23, 2017. http://www.victorianweb.org /victorian/science/addiction/addiction2.html.

DrugAbuse.com. "The Effects of Opiate Use." Retrieved September 29, 2017. https://drugabuse.com/library /the-effects-of-opiate-use.

DrugAbuse.com. "The Effects of Opiates on Your Body." Retrieved September 27, 2017. https://drugabuse.com /featured/the-effects-of-opiates-on-the-body.

DrugAbuse.com. "The Forefathers of Modern Illicit Drugs." Retrieved September 20, 2017. https://drugabuse.com /the-forefathers-of-modern-illicit-drugs.

Drug Enforcement Administration. "Drug Schedules." Retrieved September 30, 2017. https://www.dea.gov/druginfo/ds.shtml.

Garner, Anne. "'FEAR Narcotic Drugs!' The Passage of the Harrison Act." New York Academy of Medicine. Retrieved September 28, 2017. https://nyamcenterforhistory .org/2014/12/17/fear-narcotic-drugs-the-passage-of -the-harrison-act.

Gora, Gordon. "10 Historical Figures Who Were Dependent on Opium." Listverse, September 25, 2015. http://listverse .com/2015/09/25/10-historical-figures-who-were -dependent-on-opium.

Hattenstone, Simon. "Drew Barrymore: 'My Mother Locked Me Up in an Institution at 13. Boo Hoo! I Needed It.'" *Guardian*, October 25, 2015. https://www.theguardian.com /culture/2015/oct/25/drew-barrymore-mother-locked-up-in -institution-interview.

Heigl, Alex. "A Thorough Timeline of Corey Feldman's Ups and Downs." *People*, September 19, 2016. http://people.com /celebrity/corey-feldman-a-timeline-of-the-actors-ups -and-downs.

Holland, Kimberly. "10 Celebrities with Heroin Addictions."
Healthline, May 22, 2017. https://www.healthline.com/health
/celebrities-heroin-addiction#4.

Jenkins, Nash P. "Heroin Addiction's Fraught History." *Atlantic*,
February 24, 2014. https://www.theatlantic.com/health
/archive/2014/02/heroin-addictions-fraught-history/284001.

Kleinman, Zoe. "Ada Lovelace: Opium, Maths and the Victorian
Programmer." BBC, October 12, 2015. http://www.bbc.com
/news/technology-34505896.

Kolhatkar, Sheelah. "The Cost of the Opioid Crisis." *New Yorker*,
September 18, 2017. https://www.newyorker.com
/magazine/2017/09/18/the-cost-of-the-opioid-crisis.

Lee, John. "15 Signs Your Opioid Use Is Becoming Opioid
Abuse." Choose Help, April 7, 2015. http://www.choosehelp
.com/topics/opioid-addiction-pain/15-signs-that
-opioid-use-is-becoming-opioid-abuse.

MacLaren, Erik. "Heroin History and Statistics." DrugAbuse.com.
Retrieved September 20, 2017. https://drugabuse.com
/library/heroin-history-and-statistics.

Miroff, Nick. "'The Greatest Drug Fields in the World': An American
Opioid Crisis—in 1908." *Washington Post*, September 29,
2017. https://www.washingtonpost.com/news/retropolis
/wp/2017/09/29/the-greatest-drug-fiends-in-the-world-an
-american-opioid-crisis-in-1908.

Mnookin, Seth. "Why Philip Seymour Hoffman's Death Is So
Scary." Slate, February 4, 2014. http://www.slate.com
/articles/health_and_science/medical_examiner/2014/02
/philip_seymour_hoffman_s_drug_death_the_science_of
_addiction_recovery_and.html.

Moghe, Sonia. "Opioid History: From 'Wonder Drug' to Abuse
Epidemic." CNN, October 14, 2016. http://www.cnn

.com/2016/05/12/health/opioid-addiction-history /index.html.

NAACP. "Criminal Justice Fact Sheet." Retrieved September 28, 2017. http://www.naacp.org/criminal-justice-fact-sheet.

National Institute on Drug Abuse. "Opioid Crisis." Retrieved September 20, 2017. https://www.drugabuse.gov/drugs -abuse/opioids/opioid-crisis.

National Institute of Mental Health. "Brain Basics." Retrieved September 20, 2017. https://www.nimh.nih.gov/health /educational-resources/brain-basics/brain-basics.shtml.

Opiate Addiction and Treatment Resource. "Types of Opioids." Retrieved September 28, 2017. http://www .opiateaddictionresource.com/opiates/types_of_opioids.

PBS Frontline. "Opium Throughout History." Retrieved September 22, 2017. http://www.pbs.org/wgbh/pages/frontline/shows /heroin/etc/history.html.

Sanchez, Ray. "Coroner: Philip Seymour Hoffman Died of Acute Mixed Drug Intoxication." CNN, February 28, 2014. http:// www.cnn.com/2014/02/28/showbiz/philip-seymour -hoffman-autopsy/index.html.

Stanford University. "The United States War on Drugs." Retrieved September 28, 2017. https://web.stanford.edu/class/e297c /poverty_prejudice/paradox/htele.html.

Vancouver Sun. "Opioids: How They Trick the Brain to Make You Feel Good." June 2, 2014. http://www.vancouversun .com/Opioids+they+trick+brain+make+feel+good+with+vi deo/9894363/story.html.

Winton, Richard. "Autopsy Finds Child Actor Corey Haim Died of Pneumonia." Los Angeles Times, May 5, 2010. http://articles .latimes.com/2010/may/05/local/la-me-0505-corey -haim-20100505.

INDEX

ABOUT THE AUTHOR

Bethany Bryan is the author of several books for Rosen and Cavendish Publishing, an editor, and a copy editor. She is a strong advocate for therapy and self-care and urges people to seek the help they need. She lives in Kansas City.

PHOTO CREDITS

Cover WayHome Studio/Shutterstock.com; p. 5 Elisabetta Villa /Getty Images; pp. 7, 16, 28, 37, 46 FabrikaSimf /Shutterstock.com; p. 8 Pedro Pardo/AFP/Getty Images; p. 10 Fred Tanneau/AFP/Getty Images; p. 12 Brendan Smialowski /AFP/Getty Images; p. 15 Spencer Platt/Getty Images; p. 17 KidStock/Blend Images/Getty Images; p. 18 Alfred Pasieka /Science Photo Library/Getty Images; p. 21 Bayside/StockFood Creative/Getty Images; p. 23 Ulrike Schmitt-Hartmann/Taxi /Getty Images; p. 25 Caiaimage/Robert Daly/OJO+ /Getty Images; p. 29 Steve Debenport/E+/Getty Images; p. 30 Hannah Foslien/Getty Images; p. 31 Frazer Harrison /Getty Images; p. 32 Dimitrios Kambouris/Getty Images for Glamour; p. 38 Godong/Universal Images Group/Getty Images; p. 40 Bettmann/Getty Images; p. 42 CQ Archive/CQ-Roll Call Group/Getty Images; p. 47 Drew Angerer/Getty Images; p. 50 Holos/Taxi/Getty Images.

Design and Layout: Nicole Russo-Duca; Editor and Photo Researcher: Elizabeth Schmermund